CONTENTS

i

SUMMARY OF RESULTS

Pakistani municipalities are important entities in the delivery of key public services. These services include solid waste disposal, drinking water supply, education, and health facilities. However, the low quality of municipal services delivery in Pakistan has contributed to the country's poor social indicators and lack of citizen confidence in government.

To help improve municipal services, in February 2011 USAID/Pakistan signed a 5-year agreement with Khyber Pakhtunkhwa Province's Planning and Development Department (the grantee) to carry out the Khyber Pakhtunkhwa Municipal Services Program (the program). The goal of the program is the improvement of municipal service delivery to better address the basic needs of citizens located in small and medium-sized towns in Khyber Pakhtunkhwa. Because of the limited scope of resources in comparison to needs, the program was to focus on a few essential urban services, starting with safe water, sanitation, and solid waste collection and disposal. Sixty percent of the funds were to be used to implement municipal infrastructure upgrades. The rest will go toward building the government's capacity, community engagement, management systems reform, and project management. One year after signing the initial agreement, USAID/Pakistan and the grantee signed an amended agreement to extend the completion date by a few months to September 30, 2016.

USAID agreed to provide the grantee with up to $84.75 million in direct government-to-government (G2G) assistance. The mission budgeted an additional $5.25 million to fund direct agreements between USAID and outside contractors (for design, planning, monitoring and evaluation oversight) as well as account for USAID direct expense costs. In addition, the grantee agreed to contribute a total of $12.71 million over the life of the program. Therefore, the total budget is $102.71 million. USAID/Pakistan and the grantee agreed that the program would focus activities in three Divisions of the Khyber Pakhtunkhwa Province: Dera Ismail Khan, Malakand, and Peshawar. As of March 31, 2014, USAID/Pakistan had obligated $63.7 million and disbursed $8.7 million under the program for G2G assistance and other expenses incurred by outside contractors as well as USAID.

USAID's Office of Inspector General (OIG) in Pakistan conducted this audit to determine whether the Khyber Pakhtunkhwa Municipal Services Program was achieving its goal of improving selected municipal infrastructure.

Three years after the signing of the initial agreement and 2 years after the amended agreement, the program was not achieving its goal. Only a few small activities have been completed in Peshawar, such as the rehabilitation of four water supply systems, the cleaning of drains in 12 areas, and the procurement of various solid waste management vehicles and equipment. As of March 31, 2014, the mission had disbursed only $4.9 million (or 5.8 percent) of the $84.75 million in direct G2G assistance funds.

The audit disclosed the following weaknesses:

- The program has not achieved significant results (page 4). The mission agreed to contribute $84.75 million to the grantee to fund municipal infrastructure projects focusing on essential services such as sanitation, safe water and solid waste collection and disposal. These infrastructure projects would take place in the Khyber-Pakhtunkhwa divisions of Dera Ismail Khan, Malakand and Peshawar. Three years after signing the agreement, the project has

1

not achieved any significant results. Only a few small projects in the city of Peshawar have been completed. Furthermore, only $4.9 million (or 5.8 percent) of the grant agreement had been disbursed. This was caused because the mission did not actively engage and work closely with the grantee, which lacks significant capacity.

- No activities were planned for two of the three provincial divisions (page 6). The initial and amended activity agreements state the geographic focus of the program will be in the Khyber Pakhtunkhwa Divisions of Dera Ismail Khan, Malakand and Peshawar. However, no activities have been started or planned in either the Malakand or Dera Ismail Khan Divisions. Mission officials stated that then-Secretary of State Hillary Clinton directed USAID/Pakistan to focus activities in the city of Peshawar. However, no supporting documentation was provided to support this statement.

- The mission did not have an agreement with the Government of Khyber Pakhtunkhwa for earmarked funds (page 7). USAID/Pakistan received $65 million in congressionally earmarked funds, designated for drinking water projects. The mission subsequently decided to use $50 million of those earmarked funds exclusively for the city of Peshawar. However, the mission subobligated these funds along with Municipal Services Program funds, leading to confusion among mission personnel as to the geographic focus of the program. Furthermore, the mission does not have an agreement that details the original earmarked purpose.

- The mission did not conduct an environmental examination promptly (page 8). While the mission was operating under an approved umbrella Initial Environmental Examination, the project identified the need to rehabilitate two wastewater treatment plants in Peshawar. However, the required environmental examination was not completed for this specific activity for over a year, at which time it was determined that a more extensive Environmental Assessment had to be conducted. This was because the mission relied on the umbrella examination and was not actively engaged in the project. As a result, work on the wastewater treatment plants stopped.

- The Urban Policy Unit was not functioning as planned (page 9). As part of the program's activities, USAID/Pakistan agreed to fund the establishment of the Urban Policy Unit, whose purpose is to improve urban governance and development. However, 6 months past the completion date, the unit is still not fully staffed or functioning.

- The mission did not have a gender analysis process in place (page 11). A key component of gender analysis is the examination of whether females and males have access to the same public services. The mission approved the construction of public toilets at two separate locations in Peshawar. At each location, this will include 6 toilets for women, 24 (or four times as many) for men, and one toilet for the disabled. The mission could not provide any supporting analysis in determining how this construction allocation decision was reached.

To address these issues, we recommend that USAID/Pakistan:

1. Make a written justification on whether to continue the program or put the remaining $79 million to better use (page 6).

2. Implement a written action plan to address the lack of significant progress being made if the program is continued, and a written determination of whether additional capacity-building activities should be conducted (page 6).

3. Work with the Government of Khyber Pakhtunkhwa to implement a joint process of identifying and selecting infrastructure projects for the program (page 6).

4. Complete and approve a monitoring and evaluation (M&E) plan, which integrates specific approved infrastructure projects (page 6).

5. Either work with the Government of Khyber Pakhtunkhwa and document a process to start selecting municipal service infrastructure projects in the divisions of Dera Ismail Khan and Malakand, or amend the geographic scope of the activity agreement to focus on Peshawar (page 7).

6. Determine how much of the $84.75 million grant agreement pertains to water earmarked funding, separate this funding from the Municipal Services Program, and document the results (page 8).

7. Implement a separate agreement with the Government of Khyber Pakhtunkhwa regarding the water earmarked funding, outlining fund requirements (page 8).

8. Develop a process of scheduling and completing initial environmental examinations (IEEs) once specific infrastructure activities are approved (page 9).

9. Complete the environmental assessment for two wastewater treatment plants in Peshawar (page 9).

10. Implement a logical framework to understand how Urban Policy Unit activities will contribute towards the Municipal Services Program goal. If they do not, the remaining funds totaling approximately $1.6 million not spent under Project Implementation Letters 2 and 4 should be reprogrammed for better use and the results documented (page 11).

11. Establish and implement a system to assess gender considerations for individual infrastructure projects, including the preparation of gender-sensitive planning and monitoring procedures (page 12).

12. Work with the grantee to document the basis for the current allocation of toilets by gender, modify the allocation if necessary, and document the results (page 12).

Detailed findings follow. The audit's scope and methodology appear in Appendix I. Management comments are included in Appendix II, and our evaluation of these comments is included on page 13.

AUDIT FINDINGS

Program Has Not Achieved Significant Results

The activity agreement states that the project will work to provide sustainable improvement in municipal service delivery to address the basic needs of citizens located in small and medium-sized towns of Khyber Pakhtunkhwa. This would be done through infrastructure projects focusing on essential services such as sanitation, safe drinking water, and solid waste collection and disposal. While specific projects are not listed, the agreement states that USAID and the grantee, Government of Khyber Pakhtunkhwa, will jointly identify specific projects to be financed and outline these in subsequent project implementation letters. The program would focus these activities in the three priority Divisions of Dera Ismail Khan, Malakand, and Peshawar. USAID's total contribution to the grantee under the program is not to exceed $84.75 million in direct G2G assistance over a 5-year period, ending in September 2016.

USAID/Pakistan's Mission Order 200.2[1] emphasizes the consideration of risk as well as capacity of the implementing institution. It also requires mission personnel to be highly engaged with the partner government. Furthermore, in July 2014 USAID updated ADS 220 on G2G assistance, which also emphasized the importance of risk consideration, capacity of the implementing institution, and engagement.

Three years after signing the agreement, the program has not achieved any significant results. The following projects have been completed, all within the city of Peshawar:

- Rehabilitation of the water supply system in one section of the city that included repairs to pump houses, repairs or replacing leaking water supply pipelines, and various electrical or mechanical works.

- Cleaning drains in 12 locations.

- Procurement of solid waste management equipment, such as garbage compactors, mini-dumpsters, and handcarts.

The same types of projects are also in progress in other areas of the city, and the program is building public toilets in two separate locations.

However, no activities were planned or are in progress in the rest of Peshawar Division or in Dera Ismail Khan and Malakand. As of March 31, 2014, 3 years into the grant, the mission had signed seven project implementation letters with the grantee totaling $8.7 million and disbursed $4.9 million (or 5.8 percent) of the total direct G2G assistance funds.

This lack of significant progress was caused because the mission did not actively engage and work closely with the grantee. While mission officials could not definitively explain why, the audit's explanation is the mission was treating the agreement with the Government of Khyber

---

[1] USAID/Pakistan Mission Order 200.2, "Government-To-Government Assistance," was issued on June 27, 2012. The mission used this order to supplement applicable ADS policy guidance on G2G assistance, which was still in development.

Pakhtunkhwa as a standard grant and not as a G2G grant. USAID is prohibited from being substantially involved in standard grant agreements,[2] However, this is not the case with G2G grants. G2G grants work directly through a host country's government system to achieve desired outcomes, therefore its higher-level goals is to increase the institutional capacity of those systems. This can only be done through close cooperation with host country institutions, which require active engagement by mission staff to achieve success. However, such engagement was lacking on the mission's part.

The mission's unwillingness to work closely with the grantee is demonstrated in the following four areas listed below:

Project Selection Process – The agreement states that "the Parties will jointly identify specific projects to be financed under this Activity Agreement through subsequent project implementation letters, which will detail specific terms and conditions for financing projects related to the Activity." However, the mission's Federally Administered Tribal Areas / Khyber Pakhtunkhwa (FATA/KP) technical office has not worked with the grantee to establish a joint process of identifying and selecting specific infrastructure projects to fund. Instead, the mission relied on the grantee's Project Steering Committee and Project Management Unit to identify and select infrastructure projects.

Monitoring and Evaluation (M&E) Plan – Without an efficient joint process of determining specific infrastructure activities, a monitoring and evaluation plan (including indicators, baseline and target data) that analyzes performance of the activities the program will undertake cannot be developed or utilized in the management of those activities. As of February 2014—3 years after signing the initial activity agreement—the program did not have a completed or approved M&E plan (despite the ADS requirement[3] that it have one). Instead, the mission directed the grantee to develop a M&E plan, as required in the grant agreement. Although the FATA/KP technical office has a designated M&E specialist, he said he was only to facilitate the M&E process. Instead, the mission hired an outside contractor, Associates in Development, to start working with the grantee to develop an M&E plan for the program in 2014.

Gender Specialist – As discussed further in a separate finding, the mission did not work with the grantee to assess gender considerations for individual infrastructure projects. Instead, the mission placed the burden of addressing these issues on the grantee itself. The mission should have realized that such expertise would be extremely difficult for the grantee to acquire. This is despite the fact that the mission had a full-time gender specialist to address such concerns.

Environmental Assessment – As discussed further in a separate finding, the mission failed to promptly conduct a USAID required environmental assessment for the rehabilitation of two wastewater treatment plants in the city of Peshawar. This has caused a significant delay in the completion of this planned activity.

While the mission has issued awards to various firms to strengthen grantee capacity in specific areas, the lack of significant progress indicates that the capacity building efforts may not be sufficient in quality, quantity, or discipline to accomplish the goals set forth by the program. Additional capacity building efforts could provide stronger support to the program if the mission

---

[2] ADS 303.3.11, "Substantial Involvement and Cooperative Agreements."
[3] ADS 203.3.4, "Project Monitoring and Evaluation (M&E) Plans."

makes a determination to continue with the program in lieu of canceling the grant and putting the remaining funds to better use.

Although the program is being implemented through a G2G grant, superficial involvement by mission staff and the need for strengthened capacity building has led to a deficiency in program progress. If the mission does not take a more active role in working with the grantee—as is required for a G2G grant—not much will be accomplished and the citizens of Khyber Pakhtunkhwa will not receive better public services such as sanitation, safe drinking water, and solid waste collection and disposal, as was originally intended. We therefore make the following recommendations.

> *Recommendation 1. We recommend that USAID/Pakistan make a written justification whether to continue the Khyber Pakhtunkhwa Municipal Services Program or to cancel it and put the remaining funds totaling approximately $79 million to better use.*

> *Recommendation 2. We recommend that if USAID/Pakistan resolves to continue the Khyber Pakhtunkhwa Municipal Services Program, it must implement a written action plan to address the lack of significant progress being made and make a written determination of whether additional capacity-building activities should be conducted.*

> *Recommendation 3. We recommend that USAID/Pakistan work with the Government of Khyber Pakhtunkhwa to implement a joint process of identifying and selecting infrastructure projects for the program to fund.*

> *Recommendation 4. We recommend that USAID/Pakistan complete and approve a monitoring and evaluation plan, which integrates specific approved infrastructure projects.*

No Activities Were Planned for Two of Three Provincial Divisions

The initial activity agreement, dated February 2011, along with the amended activity agreement, dated February 2012, state that the geographic focus of the Municipal Services Program will be in the Dera Ismail Khan, Malakand, and Peshawar Divisions of Khyber Pakhtunkhwa Province.

However, no activities have been started or planned in Dera Ismail Khan, Malakand, and much of Peshawar. Furthermore, the director of the Project Management Unit said USAID has not shown any willingness to work in these divisions. While there had been a few joint discussions about starting activities in Dera Ismail Khan and Malakand, to date nothing has been selected or approved. Nonetheless, an official in the mission's FATA/KP technical office stated, "The geographic focus of the program still remains the same and includes the divisions of Dera Ismail Khan and Malakand. Peshawar city has been on top of the list for being a Secretary Clinton initiative."

The contrast between the stated geographic scope of the program and its actual implementation illustrates a deviation on the part of the mission. Various mission employees attributed this divergence to then-Secretary of State Hillary Clinton who directed USAID/Pakistan to focus the activities within the city of Peshawar. However, they could not give us any documentation to support this statement.

Because the program has focused activities only in Peshawar city, it will not achieve its goal of improving selected municipal infrastructure needs for the people living in the Dera Ismail Khan or Malakand Divisions. We therefore make the following recommendation.

> **Recommendation 5.** *We recommend that USAID/Pakistan either work with the Government of Khyber Pakhtunkhwa and document a process to start selecting municipal service infrastructure projects in the divisions of Dera Ismail Khan and Malakand, or amend the geographic scope of the activity agreement to focus on Peshawar.*

Mission Did Not Have an Agreement With the Government of Khyber Pakhtunkhwa for Earmarked Funds

ADS 220.3.2, "Required Procedures for Assessment and Use of Partner Country Systems," states that project design must include the selection of the appropriate obligating instrument. USAID initially will obligate funds through broadly defined bilateral agreements. Then at the program level, they are subobligated under a project level agreement. ADS 621.3.4 (a), "Types of Obligations and Documentary Evidence," states that the minimum documentation required for establishing the validity of a grant to a foreign government is the grant agreement itself, signed by both parties.

In addition to the funds the program received as part of the Enhanced Partnership with Pakistan Act,[4] the mission also received $65 million in congressionally earmarked[5] funds for drinking water projects as part of the Water for the Poor Act in 2010. It decided to make approximately $50 million available to the city of Peshawar and $15 million to Jacobabad, a city in Sindh Province.

The mission's agreement with the Government of Khyber Pakhtunkhwa for the Municipal Services Program states that USAID will provide a total estimated contribution to the grantee of $84.75 million. It does not mention congressionally earmarked drinking water funds, and the mission could not provide a separate agreement with the Government of Khyber Pakhtunkhwa pertaining to the water earmarked funds.

Subsequently, USAID internally subobligated the congressionally earmarked drinking water funds together with Municipal Service Program funds. Of the $56.8 million subobligated to the grantee under the program, $45.4 million is related directly to drinking water funds.

Water earmarked funds can only be spent on projects that meet certain policy guidance. Because that guidance is broad, however, mission officials were not clear about what specific projects are eligible for such funding. The mission therefore asks officials in Washington to clarify whether proposed infrastructure activities meet the requirements to be covered by the earmarked funds.

---

[4] The Enhanced Partnership with Pakistan Act of 2009 authorized $1.5 billion annually for five years in foreign assistance to Pakistan.

[5] An earmark is a legislative provision that directs approved funds to be spent on specific projects. The water earmark required of USAID is set by an annual appropriations act of congress. The language in the annual appropriations acts is brief, but USAID draws upon the language of the Senator Paul Simon Water for the Poor Act of 2005 (Public Law 109-121).

Because the two sources of funding have been combined under the program, this has created a misunderstanding among mission personnel that the Municipal Services Program agreement also includes water earmarked funding. This misunderstanding started in January 2011 when the mission amended their internal activity approval document for the program to include the water earmarked funding.

However, this was not followed up with an amendment to the project-level agreement with the Government of Khyber Pakhtunkhwa that accounted for the earmarked funds. Although an amended agreement between USAID and the Government of Khyber Pakhtunkhwa was signed on February 11, 2012, information on the amount of specific water earmarked funding, along with projects it could finance, was not included in this amended agreement. Mission officials stated that a separate agreement for the water earmarked funds was not required because these funds are accounted for under the broader level Pakistan Enhanced Partnership Agreement.[6] However, we believe the earmarked funds do not fall under this agreement but under the separate Water for the Poor Act.

USAID/Pakistan is unable to effectively discuss and work with the Government of Khyber Pakhtunkhwa as to how best to expend the water earmarked funds. Without this dialogue, there can be no process of selecting projects for which earmarked funding is authorized. Additionally, because it is unclear how much of the total $84.75 million in funding pertains to water earmarked funds in relation to Municipal Services Program funds, it is possible the goal, objectives, and geographic scope of the municipal services program as a whole have been impacted negatively. We therefore make the following recommendations.

> **Recommendation 6.** *We recommend that USAID/Pakistan determine how much of the $84.75 million grant agreement pertains to water earmarked funding, separate this funding from the Municipal Services Program, and document the results.*

> **Recommendation 7.** *We recommend that USAID/Pakistan implement a separate agreement with the Government of Khyber Pakhtunkhwa regarding the water earmarked funding, outlining fund requirements.*

Mission Did Not Conduct Environmental Examination Promptly

ADS 201.3.8.3.a, "Obligation by Development Objective Agreement," states that before funds are obligated, an appropriate initial environmental examination (IEE), categorical exclusion, or environmental assessment must be performed.

Initially, the program was operating on an approved umbrella IEE, dated September 27, 2010. This was approved because "specific information is not available on each possible activity as the actual infrastructure upgrade interventions will only be determined by the local communities in the participating municipalities in response to local needs and capabilities." The umbrella IEE therefore, required project specific IEE's to be conducted once the activities were approved.

---

[6] The Pakistan Enhanced Partnership Agreement is the obligating mechanism used by USAID/Pakistan for the funds received as part of the Enhanced Partnership with Pakistan Act.

The mission and Halcrow Pakistan Ltd., the contractor providing independent monitoring and oversight for infrastructure projects in Peshawar, had identified the need to rehabilitate two wastewater treatment plants as early as June 2012 under the Municipal Services Program. However, the required examination for this activity was not completed until August 5, 2013, more than 1 year later. This examination determined that such rehabilitation work could have "a moderate to severe adverse effects on the natural or physical environment" and therefore required that an official environmental assessment be conducted. Work towards rehabilitating the two wastewater treatment plants in Peshawar was then put on hold until the assessment is concluded.

Because the mission was relying on the umbrella IEE, and was not actively engaged in the progress of specific infrastructure activities, a delay in conducting the specific IEE and the subsequent Environmental Assessment for the rehabilitation of two wastewater treatment plants occurred. The infrastructure rehabilitation work has therefore been delayed until the Environmental Assessment is completed.

If the mission does not take a more active role in the progress of program activities, not much will be accomplished and the citizens of Khyber Pakhtunkhwa will not receive better public services. We therefore make the following recommendations.

> **Recommendation 8.** *We recommend that USAID/Pakistan implement a process of scheduling and completing initial environmental examinations once specific infrastructure activities are approved.*

> **Recommendation 9.** *We recommend that USAID/Pakistan complete the environmental assessment for two wastewater treatment plants in Peshawar.*

Urban Policy Unit Was Not Functioning as Planned

Under the program, the mission decided to fund the establishment of an Urban Policy Unit to support overall program goals. However, the unit was not functioning as planned, and its activities were not related to the program.

Unit Was Not Functioning As Planned. Through Project Implementation Letter 2, dated September 24, 2012, USAID agreed to provide up to $462,663 in initial funding to establish the Khyber Pakhtunkhwa Government's Urban Policy Unit. This Unit would work on "improving urban governance, management, planning and development, so that cities become more efficient." USAID funding to establish the Unit would be used to buy furniture, vehicles, and equipment. USAID agreed to provide the funds to the Government of Khyber Pakhtunkhwa on a cost-reimbursement basis, with a stated completion date of September 30, 2013.

However, the Unit was not functioning as planned. As of March 31, 2014, the mission had disbursed only $147,208 (or 32 percent) of the funds for the Unit's establishment. This money has been used to purchase seven vehicles, three motorcycles, two air conditioners, a generator, two photocopiers, two multimedia projectors, telephone network equipment, and a fax machine.

Employees at the Urban Policy Unit in Peshawar said only 50 percent of the staff has been hired. They also said the purchase of necessary office equipment such as computers, laptops, and other items should be completed by June 2014, or 9 months after the agreed-upon completion date.

The staff asserted that the delays in establishing the Unit has been caused by a variety of factors, including a temporary government hiring freeze, recruitment issues due to proposed salaries, and the slow nature of the government hiring process overall.

Eighteen months after USAID's letter supporting the establishment of the unit, and (as of March 31, 2014) 6 months past the estimated completion date, the office is still not functioning as planned, and it is uncertain that it ever will be operational.

Unit Activities Were Not Related to the Program. ADS 200.3.5.4, "Project Design and Implementation," states that a project's inputs or resources should be linked to results or outputs, which in turn are thereby linked to the program's purpose. This process is outlined in what is called a logical framework.

The Municipal Services Program is focused on improving municipal infrastructure in the areas of water, sanitation, and solid waste management. Project Implementation Letter 2 states the unit will have an overall budget of $10.1 million for activity funding. Of this, USAID will provide $6.4 million and the Government of Khyber Pakhtunkhwa will contribute $3.7 million. Project Implementation Letter 4 specified that $1.3 million of USAID's $6.4 million was to be used to support the activities listed in the table below.

Urban Policy Unit – USAID Project Implementation Letter 4
Budget Summary (Unaudited)

Activity	Total ($)
Traffic management plan for cities of Abbottabad, Kohat, Mardan, and Peshawar	220,000
Design of pedestrian precincts and parking plaza	200,000
Conference on transportation issues and other urban subjects	200,000
Workshops and trainings on urban issues	200,000
Study of urban-related laws	200,000
Study of slums in urban areas	100,000
Geometric design standards manual	50,000
Development of the Road Management Act	50,000
Public transport infrastructure improvement survey for Peshawar	50,000
Media campaign	30,000
Total	**1,300,000**

According to the activities listed above and discussion with staff at the Urban Policy Unit, their focus is on transportation issues as opposed to a focus on improving municipal infrastructure in the areas of water, sanitation, and solid waste management.

It is unclear how the Unit's activities will contribute to the program's success. Mission officials could not provide documentation showing how the unit's $10.1 million budget was developed.

According to staff at the Urban Policy Unit, the $1.3 million budgeted activities were developed entirely by the previous Executive Director. Although most of these activities do not pertain to water, sanitation, and solid waste management, they do fall under the Unit's government of Pakistan determined mandate.

Because the mission does not have a completed or approved logical framework, it is unclear how these activities will be utilized in order to contribute to the program's overall goal. Furthermore as discussed in the first finding, the mission was not actively engaged and working closely with the grantee and could not provide any information justifying why these activities were approved and how they were going to contribute to the program's overall goal.

If the Urban Policy Unit carries out the activities in the table, the mission could be spending funds that would have no impact on contributing to the program's focus areas. This includes approximately $1.6 million in undisbursed funds from Project Implementation Letters 2 and 4. We therefore make the following recommendation.

> ***Recommendation 10.*** *We recommend that USAID/Pakistan implement a logical framework to understand how Urban Policy Unit activities contribute to the Municipal Services Program's goal. If they do not, the remaining funds totaling approximately $1.6 million not spent under Project Implementation Letters 2 and 4 should be reprogrammed for better use and the results documented.*

Mission Did Not Have Gender Analysis Process in Place

ADS 201.3.4.2 (b), "Phase 2 – Results Framework Development," states that "promoting gender equality and advancing the status of women and girls around the world remains as one of the greatest unmet challenges of our time, and one that is vital to achieving U.S. development objectives." It further states that for projects, the gender analysis for the activity approval document may need to be supplemented for the design of each subordinate activity, and the responsibility for deciding whether additional gender analyses are required rests with the project team, in consultation with the relevant gender adviser.[7]

Furthermore, ADS 205[8] states that a key component of gender analysis is an examination of whether women and men have access to productive resources, such as public services. Moreover, while gender gaps in access to resources can be identified at the country level, they are especially important at the project level. Therefore, USAID technical teams and program staff must be substantially involved in the gender analysis process. Simply having a coordination function and providing a list of documents does not constitute active engagement.

The program's activity approval document states, "Pakistan remains one of the most gender unequal countries in the world. A patriarchal social framework places women in a highly vulnerable and marginalized position in the family, and in society in general." Project Implementation Letter 6 outlines various infrastructure projects in Peshawar, including one to construct public restrooms at two separate locations in Peshawar for a total cost of $326,960. Each would have 6 toilets for women, 24 toilets (or four times as many) for men, and 1 for the disabled.

Employees in the mission's technical office of FATA/KP said six for women is still a relatively

---

[7] ADS 201.3.15.3 (a), "Stage 2: Process – Analytical Stage."
[8] ADS 205.3.1, "What is Gender Analysis?"

high number and that most women in the region do not use public toilets. They said they based this decision on discussions with visitors to this area and a sanitation specialist. However, they did not provide any documentation that supported this allocation decision and the rationale behind it.

As explained in the first finding, the mission is not actively engaged with the grantee, possibly due to treating the funding mechanism like a standard grant as opposed to a G2G grant agreement. Therefore, the mission did not have a system in place to assess gender considerations for individual infrastructure projects under the program. Instead, it relied on the grantee to assess and address these concerns. Internal mission documentation stated that for gender concerns, the provincial government was charged with preparing gender-sensitive planning and monitoring procedures. These procedures would describe in detail how the grantee will make certain that women would participate in all planning, implementation, and reform efforts, and how that participation will be implemented and tracked.

Other internal mission documents show that the grantee is responsible for appointing a full-time gender adviser to address such concerns, despite the fact that the mission has a full-time gender specialist who could have been called upon to help while the search for an appropriate candidate was under way.

To date, the grantee has not been able to hire such an expert, or provide the mission with gender-sensitive planning and monitoring procedures. The mission should have realized that such expertise is not available on the local market and assisted the grantee with this requirement.

By not ensuring appropriate, fact-based gender analysis is conducted, women in the community could continue to be marginalized through lack of access to public services. We therefore make the following recommendations.

> **Recommendation 11.** *We recommend that USAID/Pakistan establish and implement a system to assess gender considerations for individual infrastructure projects, including the preparation of gender-sensitive planning and monitoring procedures.*

> **Recommendation 12.** *We recommend that USAID/Pakistan work with the grantee to document the basis for the current allocation of toilets by gender, modify the allocation if necessary, and document the results.*

EVALUATION OF MANAGEMENT COMMENTS

USAID/Pakistan generally agreed with eight recommendations in the draft report but did not believe that further action was needed for the other four recommendations in the report. According to the information the mission provided in its response to the draft report (received on January 21 and clarified on January 30), we acknowledge management decisions on Recommendations 2, 3, 4, 7, 8, 9, 10, 11, and 12, and final actions on 1, 5, and 6.

The mission provided an overview on the program's background to put the issues highlighted in the report into context. The mission highlights the importance of Peshawar city and said that in 2011 "there was substantive USG interagency review that lead to redesigning MSP in order to focus on major renovations of Peshawar, KP." The mission then states that at this time, $45.366 million in water earmarked funds were designated to the program. As the report's third finding states, these substantial changes in the program's scope were not reflected in a new agreement or an amendment to the mission's current agreement with the Government of Khyber Pakhtunkhwa.

Additionally, the mission stated they held off implementing program initiatives until after the completion of a Peshawar master plan in August 2013, which encompassed water, sanitation, and solid waste management infrastructure in the city. However, we note that on November 16, 2012 the mission awarded National Development Consultants a $4 million task order to assess the condition of the existing drinking water, sanitation/storm water, and solid waste systems in Peshawar city, which would be summarized in a master plan report. This activity was to be concluded by the award completion date of May 15, 2014, or 9 months later than the mission stated in its response. Furthermore, we did not receive a copy of the master plan to verify the completion date.

Recommendation 1. USAID/Pakistan agreed with this recommendation and stated that it will continue the program because it is in the best interest of the U.S. Government and the Government of Khyber Pakhtunkhwa.

The mission also said project implementation letters totaling $11.22 million have been signed and another $11.09 are in circulation for mission clearance, representing "40% of the total funds subobligated for the program." The figure of 40 percent presents an overly optimistic picture, because it is calculated based on the subobligated amount of $56.84 million provided by the mission. A calculation using the total amount of the grant agreement, $84.75 million, would provide a more realistic picture comparing the total amount of implementation letters either signed or in circulation. This comes to only 26 percent, 4 years after signing the 5-year grant agreement with the Government of Khyber Pakhtunkhwa. However, since the mission has decided to continue the program, final action has been taken.

Recommendation 2. USAID/Pakistan agreed and planned to take final action by June 2015. The mission provided a written action plan (annex not included in this report) and agreed to develop a plan that identifies further capacity building needs by June 2015. Accordingly, the mission has made a management decision.

Recommendation 3. USAID/Pakistan did not believe further action was needed and said that the current process for identifying and selecting infrastructure projects was adequate. The mission provided information stating that as of November 2013, $11.22 million in project implementation letters were signed; this represents only 13 percent of the total grant agreement 4 years after implementation. Based on this low percentage rate of progress, we do not consider the current process to be adequate in identifying and selecting infrastructure projects.

We determined that projects are selected by the Government of Khyber Pakhtunkhwa, which it then shared with USAID for approval. We do not consider mission approval or rejection of the host government's selected infrastructure projects to be an adequate joint collaborative process. An efficient process, in which both parties work together to determine the infrastructure projects that would bring the most value to the people of Khyber Pakhtunkhwa is needed. Such a process could also strengthen the capacity of host-government officials.

Furthermore, we believe this recommendation is explicitly linked with Recommendation 4 pertaining to a completed and approved M&E plan. A joint process of identifying and selecting infrastructure projects is necessary for an adequate M&E plan. Nonetheless, we acknowledge the mission has made a management decision although we do not consider it to be consistent with the objectives of the program or an efficient and effective methodology nor does it represent final action. Therefore, final action can be achieved when the mission provides examples of the joint collaborative process being implemented.

Recommendation 4. USAID/Pakistan agreed with this recommendation and stated that an M&E plan could not be initiated earlier because of project delays. The purpose of a USAID required M&E plan is to measure progress toward planned results and identify the cause of any delays or impediments during implementation. Therefore, if an efficient process of determining specific infrastructure activities is not in place, a meaningful M&E plan will be difficult. Nevertheless, the mission expects an approved M&E plan by March 31, 2015, or 4 years after initial program implementation. Accordingly, the mission has made a management decision.

Recommendation 5. USAID/Pakistan agreed and provided a list of three activities worth $8 million (attachment not included in this report) for Dera Ismail Khan and seven worth $15.3 million for Malakand. Therefore, we acknowledge the mission's management decision and final action.

Recommendations 6 and 7. USAID/Pakistan appreciated the intent of the recommendations but did not believe further action was needed and provided one response for both. It stated that the $45.366 million of earmarked funds are tracked separately in the mission's accounting system. It stated these funds can only be disbursed to pay for eligible activities, and the mission is required to report results against the earmarked funds by law. Since the mission has determined the amount of water earmarked funds and separately tracks these funds in their accounting system for reporting purposes, a management decision has been made and final action has taken place on Recommendation 6.

Additionally, the mission said, the grant agreement with the Government of Khyber Pakhtunkhwa covers both water and non-water activities, negating the need for a separate agreement. As the finding states, water earmarked funds are not outlined in the grant agreement with the Government of Khyber Pakhtunkhwa, which affects the program's goal, objective, and geographic scope. Regardless of whether the earmarked funds fall under the Enhanced Partnership with Pakistan Act or not, a relevant grant agreement, signed by both parties, is required. Since the mission stated that $45.366 million of the $84.75 million grant pertains to earmarked funds focused on Peshawar city, this accounts for 54 percent of total funds. Such a significant amount would justify either a separate or amended agreement with the Government of Khyber Pakhtunkhwa to more accurately reflect the funding terms. Furthermore, since the agency has the responsibility to assure optimal use of funds and adherence to congressional earmarks, a reasonable role for the mission would be to provide guidance to the Government of Khyber Pakhtunkhwa and ensure that the scopes of work and program description in awards include definitions and appropriate use of funds for activities. From a best practice perspective, this would be in line with USAID's ADS guidance on water earmarks in Global Health Programs[9].

Contrary to the management decision made by the mission for Recommendation 7, we believe that the agency guidance described clearly illustrates the importance of outlining the appropriate use of funds, such as earmarks, in awards to recipients to ensure adherence with legislative directives as well as facilitate project selection. Although we acknowledge the mission's management decision, we disagree that final action has been reached. Therefore, in order to achieve final action, the mission should demonstrate that the grantee is aware of fund requirements regarding the water earmarked funding through a new or amended agreement.

Recommendation 8. USAID/Pakistan did not believe further action was needed for this recommendation. The mission stated it was in compliance with the requirement that the environmental examination documentation is to be in place before work starts on any activity.

The finding did not dispute whether the mission was in compliance. Rather, it was not done promptly and therefore the mission should implement a process of scheduling and completing such examinations promptly to reduce unnecessary delays. Although we acknowledge the mission's management decision, we disagree that final action has been reached. To achieve final action, the mission should include the above-mentioned process as part of its M&E plan, which is planned for completion by March 31, 2015.

Recommendation 9. The mission stated that the environmental assessment for the wastewater treatment plants in Peshawar would be completed by March 2015. Accordingly, the mission has made a management decision.

Recommendation 10. The mission stated that a logical framework for the Urban Policy Unit activities would be completed by March 31, 2015. Accordingly, the mission has made a management decision.

Recommendation 11. The mission agreed with the recommendation and planned to take final action by March 31, 2015. Accordingly, the mission has made a management decision.

Recommendation 12. The mission agreed with the recommendation and planned to take final action by March 31, 2015. Accordingly, the mission has made a management decision.

---

[9] Guidance on the Definition and Use of the Global Health Programs Account, A Mandatory Reference for ADS Chapter 200

SCOPE AND METHODOLOGY

Scope

OIG/Pakistan conducted this performance audit in accordance with generally accepted government auditing standards. They require that we plan and perform the audit to obtain sufficient, appropriate evidence to provide a reasonable basis for our findings and conclusions in accordance with our audit objectives. We believe the evidence obtained provides that reasonable basis.

We based our conclusions on sources of information reviewed during the audit. These sources included interviews with staff from USAID/Pakistan, Khyber Pakhtunkhwa Government officials, and contractors involved in the program. Discussions took place in Islamabad and Peshawar.

The objective of this audit was to determine whether the Khyber Pakhtunkhwa Municipal Services Program was achieving its goal of improving selected municipal infrastructure. We conducted audit fieldwork from December 9, 2013, to April 30, 2014, at USAID/Pakistan's office in Islamabad; at the Government of Khyber Pakhtunkhwa's Program Management Unit; and at the offices of Halcrow Pakistan, Ltd. We also visited infrastructure activities in the city of Peshawar. The audit covered the period from February 11, 2011, to March 31, 2014.

As of March 31, 2014, USAID/Pakistan has obligated $63.7 million and disbursed $8.7 million under the program.

In planning and performing the audit, the audit team assessed controls the mission used to manage the program and ensure adequate oversight of program activities. These controls included those regarding coordination with Khyber Pakhtunkhwa Government officials and implementers. Specifically, we examined and evaluated internal control documentation prepared by the mission, the provincial government, and contractors, such as the following:

- Agreement between the Khyber Pakhtunkhwa Government and USAID

- Government of Pakistan's Planning Commission document known as the PC-1

- Project implementation letters

- USAID/Pakistan vouchers

- USAID contracts with Halcrow and National Development Consultants

- Earmarked funding legislation

We also reviewed certain mission oversight processes, such as voucher approval, portfolio reviews, and how activities are determined to meet the water earmarked funding criteria.

Methodology

To answer the audit objective, we first reviewed all applicable documents pertaining to the program. This included reviewing such documents as the grant agreement between USAID/Pakistan and the Government of Khyber Pakhtunkhwa, project implementation letters, contracts between USAID/Pakistan and private contractors, work plans, monthly and quarterly progress reports, applicable regulations (such as USAID's ADS and USAID/Pakistan mission orders), and related OIG audit reports. The audit team also conducted interviews in Islamabad with officials from the mission, Government of Khyber Pakhtunkhwa's project management unit, Halcrow Pakistan, Ltd., National Development Consultants, and Associates in Development.

Through the documentation reviews and interviews, the audit team obtained an understanding of (1) the program's goals, (2) program design and planning, (3) monitoring of activities, (4) accomplishments to date, and (5) whether the mission or program partners were aware of any allegations of fraud, other potential illegal acts, or noncompliance with laws and regulations.

The audit team planned to test a sample of reported results data. However, because no baseline or target data were established, and minimal results had been reported, no sampling was conducted. To verify the results reported to date and understand why the program did not have any significant achievements to date, the audit team conducted a 2-day site visit in Peshawar; we chose this city because it was the only place where projects were active or completed. We also met with project stakeholders and beneficiaries.

MANAGEMENT COMMENTS

MEMORANDUM

Date	January 7, 2015
To	William Murphy- Director/OIG Pakistan
From	Nancy Estes- Acting Mission Director USAID/Pakistan
Subject	Management Decision on the Performance Audit of USAID/Pakistan's Khyber Pakhtunkhwa Municipal Services Program (MSPKP)
Reference	Draft Audit Report No. G-391-15-00X- P dated Nov 14, 2014

The USAID/Pakistan Mission would like to thank the USAID Office of Inspector General (OIG) for providing the Mission the opportunity to review and provide comments to the draft performance audit report covering the Khyber Pakhtunkhwa Municipal Services Program (MSPKP).

The Mission's engagement with the Government of the Khyber Pakhtunkhwa (GoKP) province in the planning and implementation of MSPKP, as well as its overall management of the program, has been rigorous from the start. USAID and Department of State field personnel, both staff and senior leadership, continue a collaborative engagement with GoKP to meet the objectives of the program. Despite the acknowledged delays in completing MSPKP as currently designed, significant achievements have been made. As a result of the activities undertaken by MSPKP, a new government-owned company called Water and Sanitation Services Peshawar (WSSP) has been established to replace several departments of GoKP providing water supply, sanitation, and solid waste management services in Peshawar city. Due to the success of this intervention, the GoKP is now planning to replicate it for other major cities of the province. Furthermore, in spite of the delays encountered in getting the program activities off the ground, approximately 714,000 residents of Peshawar city have benefited from the program activities completed as of this audit response. All primary and secondary drains in the downtown 25 union councils of Peshawar have been cleared of silt. 24 kilometers of old and damaged pipes of the drinking water distribution system have been replaced. Improvement of primary and secondary drains in four union councils is underway, and 7 kilometers of drains have been improved or rehabilitated as of December 31, 2014. Electro-mechanical equipment replacement and civil works renovation has been completed for 40 water supply systems (tube wells). In addition, solid waste management equipment, machinery, and vehicles have been provided for use in 12 union councils of Peshawar city, which has markedly improved the solid waste collection system. USAID/Pakistan therefore seeks the opportunity to discuss and provide additional information to the OIG as necessary in order to ensure the final audit report accurately describes the Mission's fulsome engagement with GoKP, its active management of MSPKP, and the program's significant results to date.

We also take this opportunity to provide a brief historical background of the overall Municipal Services Program (MSP) and of its MSPKP component which is the subject of this audit.

The MSP was originally established on July 9, 2010, as a governance program focused on municipal reform, to be implemented in all four provinces of Pakistan- Punjab, Sindh, Balochistan, and KP. By mid-2011 there was substantive USG interagency review that led to redesigning MSP in order to focus on major renovations of Peshawar, KP and Jacobabad, Sindh municipal water systems, and the cessation of active work on Balochistan and Punjab components. During this period, FY 2010 MSP funding of $65 million was designated for use in meeting USAID's agency water earmark, of which, $45.366 million was allocated to MSPKP. The Activity Agreement between the Mission and the GoKP was amended February 11, 2012, to sub-obligate these funds.

Peshawar city has a significant importance for the Government of Pakistan (GoP). Peshawar has been hosting a significant number of Afghan refugees ever since Russia invaded Afghanistan. During the last 10 years the city has been absorbing the bulk of Internally Displaced Persons (IDPs) from the Federally Administered Tribal Areas (FATA), and has faced substantial security incidents as a result of retaliation from militants. For the GoP, Peshawar has been a front line with regards to its war on terrorism, and consequently the city has suffered grave damages and losses, greater than any other part of the country. These conditions continue to strain municipal service delivery and underscore the importance of MSPKP.

With the support of the Mission, the GoKP initiated the design of a Master Plan for Peshawar water, sanitation, and solid waste management infrastructure in October 2011, which was necessary to drive the design of appropriate municipal activities. The Master Plan was not completed until August of 2013. Accordingly, the Mission held off on implementing major infrastructure initiatives until after the Master Plan was completed, which helps to explain the significant delay. In the interim, the focus was on smaller infrastructure initiatives, particularly solid waste management. While the Master Plan took time, the Mission believes the Plan was necessary to ensure the best use of resources to successfully complete MSPKP.

In 2013, the program experienced further delay. When designs of two water treatment plants were completed, the USAID Environmental Officer communicated that a full-fledged Environmental Assessment (EA) was required for the treatment plants. The EA is currently underway and the final report will be available by March 31, 2015. While Annex A to this response indicates MSPKP will complete by the end of 2016, the Mission is considering whether circumstances now indicate a completion date in 2017.

The Mission requests that the final audit report delete recommendation 7, which recommends that the Mission implement a separate agreement with the GoKP regarding the water earmarked funding, outlining fund requirements. That recommendation appears to be based on the assumption that earmarked water funds are separate from Economic Support Funds (ESF) authorized pursuant to KLB, which they are not. The water earmark does put limits on how to use some of the funds in order to be attributed to that earmark, but there is no separate funding stream other than ESF. Moreover, please note that the Mission does have a system in place to separately track earmark funds both from an accounting and performance standpoint, and therefore the Mission requests closure of Recommendation 6, which calls for the Mission to determine how much of the $84.75 million grant agreement pertains to water earmarked funding (which is known), separate this funding from the Municipal Services Program (which is not required), and document the results

Please find below additional specific comments to the recommendations included in the draft audit report.

Recommendation No. 1: We recommend that USAID/Pakistan make a written justification whether to continue the Khyber Pakhtunkhwa Municipal Services Program or to cancel it and put the remaining funds totaling approximately $79 million to better use.

Management Comments

The Mission agrees with the intent of the recommendation and has determined that it is in the best interests of the United States Government and the GoKP to continue the Municipal Services Program in Khyber Pakhtunkhwa.

Khyber Pakhtunkhwa province has faced enormous challenges in recent years. The province has been host to thousands of Afghan refugees for more than three decades. The province has also experienced rapid population growth and migrations from militancy-affected areas to urban areas, especially to the city of Peshawar. These have put tremendous pressure on aging and insufficient infrastructure for essential municipal services, such as for water supply, sanitation, and solid waste management. Coupled with poor urban planning and obsolete operational and information management systems, these have resulted in insufficient and highly unreliable service provision. To address these challenges, MSPKP focuses on investing in municipal services infrastructure, improving local governance and management systems, enhancing capacities of service providers, and encouraging ownership by local communities. Improving municipal service delivery benefits the people of KP province and builds public trust and support for local government institutions, which in turn promotes greater stability in this unsettled region. The Mission has worked with the GoKP to develop the attached Action Plan (see Annex A) for the project which provides details of activities undertaken to date and the status of activities planned for the future along with target completion dates. The current financial status of the program is summarized as follows.

The estimated budget ceiling of the grant to the GoKP for implementation of MSPKP is $84.75 million. The current sub-obligation under the MSPKP Activity Agreement stands at $56.84 million, of which $45.366 million is the water earmark allocation. Project Implementation Letters (PILs) worth $11.22 million have been signed and another three for a total of $11.09 million are in circulation for clearances at the Mission. These together represent around 40% of the total funds sub-obligated for the program. Specific activities have been planned to be funded with the balance of $34.5 million (60%) which is already sub-obligated. The Action Plan for the $34.5 million (60%) has been shared through Annex- A referred above.

In addition to continued program management and liaison with the GoKP by the Mission, MSPKP will continue to be part of regular Mission portfolio reviews and performance reporting, to help ensure reasonable progress is being made and the program is successfully completed.

In view of the information provided above and elsewhere in response to the draft audit, the Mission reports that the final action has been taken and requests closure of this recommendation upon issuance of the final audit report.

Recommendation No. 2: We recommend that if USAID/Pakistan resolves to continue the Khyber Pakhtunkhwa Municipal Services Program, it must implement a written action plan to address the lack of significant progress being made and make a written determination of whether additional capacity-building activities should be conducted.

Management Comments

Having resolved to continue the Khyber Pakhtunkhwa Municipal Services Program based on the significant progress being made under the evolved context and conditions of the activity, the Mission agrees with the recommendation to develop an action plan to identify further capacity building needs.

Capacity building activities for operational as well as programmatic functions have been ongoing since the inception of the project. These interventions have been validated and positive results have been achieved. In addition, we agree to develop a plan identifying further capacity building needs and the proposed actions to meet such requirements by June 2015. Please refer to Annex A for USAID/Pakistan's action plan which includes target dates for signing of Project Implementation Letters (PILs) of specific activities for the remaining period of the project.

Recommendation No. 3: We recommend that USAID/Pakistan work with the Government of Khyber Pakhtunkhwa to implement a joint process of identifying and selecting infrastructure projects for the program to fund.

Management Comments

An adequate joint process for identifying and selecting infrastructure projects for the program was already in place prior to the audit and has since remained in place. If this recommendation is retained in the final audit report, we request closure of this recommendation upon issuance of the final audit report.

To further clarify, the Activity Agreement for the MSPKP program specifically spells out how projects are to be jointly selected. Project Implementation Letters (PILs) provide information on the design and specifications, funding, payment arrangements, and other details necessary for implementation of the projects jointly selected by USAID and the GoKP.

Recommendation No. 4: We recommend that USAID/Pakistan complete and approve a monitoring and evaluation plan, which integrates specific approved infrastructure projects.

Management Comments

The Mission agrees with this recommendation. The work on preparation of the MSPKP Monitoring and Evaluation (M&E) plan could not be initiated earlier because of the delays in the project launch, but it is now in an advanced draft stage. (Even in the absence of a formal M&E plan, a three tier mechanism for the monitoring of activities implemented under MSPKP was in place from the start of the program activities.) The draft M&E plan is currently under review by the Mission's Performance Management Unit. The Mission expects the approved M&E plan to be in place by March 31, 2015. Specific approved infrastructure activities to be implemented under MSPKP will be integrated in the M&E plan.

Recommendation No. 5: We recommend that USAID/Pakistan either work with the Government of Khyber Pakhtunkhwa and document a process to start selecting municipal service infrastructure projects in the divisions of Dera Ismail Khan and Malakand, or amend the geographic scope of the activity agreement to focus on Peshawar.

Management Comments

The Mission agrees with the intent of this recommendation and reports that GoKP has already identified activities in Dera Ismail Khan and Malakand divisions which are documented under the attached Action Plan provided as Annex A1. These activities are currently under review at the Mission. In view of the above, the Mission reports that the final action has already been taken and requests closure of this recommendation upon issuance of the final audit report.

Recommendation No. 6: We recommend that USAID/Pakistan determine how much of the $84.75 million grant agreement pertains to water earmarked funding, separate this funding from the Municipal Services Program, and document the results.

Recommendation No. 7: We recommend that USAID/Pakistan implement a separate agreement with the Government of Khyber Pakhtunkhwa regarding the water earmarked funding, outlining fund requirements.

Management Comments

The response below covers both Recommendations 6 and 7. The Mission appreciates the intent of these recommendations, but does not agree that the recommendations should be included in the final audit report. The Mission's Phoenix accounting system separately tracks water earmark funding and the Program Office tracks the related results (see Annex A). The Mission also confirmed with USAID's Office of the General Counsel that there is no legal requirement for Recommendation 7. Consequently, the Mission can clearly identify the split between water and non-water funds as these funds are being tracked and monitored accordingly.

The amount of water earmark funding sub-obligated for the entire Municipal Services Program, including both the Sindh and Khyber Pakhtunkhwa components of MSP, was $65 million. Of this, $45.366 million was allocated to MSPKP. This was done when the decision to focus MSP on Peshawar and Jacobabad was made. Indeed, the allocation of water earmark funds was an important determining factor on the split of MSP funds between the two cities. Earmarked funds may only be allocated and disbursed to finance eligible activities and this is tracked. The Mission is also required to report results against the earmarked funds by law, further documenting that the funds are used for eligible purposes.

Furthermore, the scope of work for MSPKP covers both water and non-water activities. Additionally, there are no water earmark funds separate from the ESF allocation the Mission received that would also be attributed to KLB, as the draft audit report suggests. Similarly, USAID does not receive funds "as part of" the Enhanced Partnership with Pakistan Act; rather the Mission received ESF funds for this program that were authorized pursuant to that Act. The water earmark does put limits on how to use the funds in order to be attributed to that earmark, but there is no separate funding stream other than ESF, nor is there a requirement for a separate agreement with the GoKP based on the existence of this earmark. Moreover, and importantly, water earmark funds have broader use than just drinking water. Of importance to MSP, wastewater management and strengthening the water management utility also qualify. The Master Plan identifies earmark qualifying activities that far exceed the available funds.

In view of the above, the Mission requests that Recommendations 6 and 7 be deleted and not included in the final audit report. If Recommendation 7 is included in the final audit report, as the Mission is already in compliance with this recommendation, the Mission requests closure upon issuance of the final audit report.

Recommendation No. 8: **We recommend that USAID/Pakistan implement a process of scheduling and completing initial environmental examinations once specific infrastructure activities are approved.**

Management Comments

The Mission is already in compliance with this recommendation. The Mission is aware of and in compliance with the requirement that the environmental examination documentation is to be in place before work commences on any activity. As noted by the audit, an umbrella Initial Environmental Examination (IEE) for MSP was approved by the Bureau Environmental Officer (BEO) on September 17, 2010. After specific activities had been identified for implementation under the program, a revised IEE was prepared by USAID/Pakistan, which was approved by the BEO on September 4, 2013. An Environmental Assessment (EA) for the rehabilitation of wastewater treatment plants in Peshawar is currently underway. It is important to note here that the work is on-going and completed activities under MSPKP did not commence until all required environmental documentation was completed and approved, and the work on the wastewater treatment plants will only commence once the EA is in place.

In view of the above, the Mission reports that no further action is required. If the recommendation is included in the final audit report then them Mission requests closure of the recommendation upon issuance of the final audit report.

Recommendation No. 9: **We recommend that USAID/Pakistan complete the environmental assessment for the two wastewater treatment plants in Peshawar.**

Management Comments

The Mission agrees with the recommendation. As mentioned in the response to Recommendation 8 above, the scoping statement for the Environmental Assessment (EA) for the wastewater treatment plants in Peshawar is being reviewed by the BEO, and the report of the EA will be available by end of March 2015.

Recommendation No. 10: **We recommend that USAID/Pakistan implement a logical framework to understand how Urban Policy Unit activities contribute to the Municipal Services Program's goal. If they do not, the remaining funds totaling approximately $1.6 million not spent under project implementation letters 2 and 4 should be reprogrammed for better use and the results documented.**

Management Comments

The Mission agrees with this recommendation. A draft logical framework and results framework for MSP is now complete and is in circulation for approval that is expected to be finalized by March 31, 2015. The mandate of the Urban Policy Unit (UPU) to the program's goal is guided by the logical and result frameworks.

Recommendation No. 11: We recommend that USAID/Pakistan establish and implement a system to assess gender considerations for individual infrastructure projects, including the preparation of gender-sensitive planning and monitoring procedures.

Management Comments

The Mission agrees with the recommendation with regards to MSPKP. Gender considerations will be incorporated in MSPKP's final approved logical framework and the monitoring and evaluation plan which are currently under review. The Mission expects to complete the related final action with respect to this recommendation by March 31, 2015.

Recommendation 12: We recommend that USAID/Pakistan work with the grantee to document the basis for the current allocation of toilets by gender, modify the allocation if necessary, and document the results.

Management Comments

The Mission agrees with this recommendation. The Mission will work with the PMU of MSPKP to document the basis for the current allocation of toilets by gender. The Mission expects to complete the final action with respect to this recommendation by March 31, 2015.